All You Need to Know About Real Estate Unleashed

By Ade Asefeso MCIPS MBA

Second Edition

ISBN-13: 978-1499600025

ISBN-10: 149960002X

Publisher: AA Global Sourcing Ltd
Website: http://www.aaglobalsourcing.com

1

Table of Contents

Disclaimer

This publication is designed to provide competent and reliable information regarding the subject matter covered. However, it is sold with the understanding that the author and publisher are not engaged in rendering professional advice. The authors and publishers specifically disclaim any liability that is incurred from the use or application of contents of this book.

Dedication

This book is dedicated to the hundreds of thousands of incredible souls in the world who have weathered through the up and down of recent recession.

To my family and friends who seems to have been sent here to teach me something about who I am supposed to be. They have nurtured me, challenged me, and even opposed me.... But at every juncture has taught me!

This book is dedicated to my lovely boys, Thomas, Michael and Karl. Teaching them to manage their finance will give them the lives they deserve. They have taught me more about life, presence, and energy management than anything I have done in my life.

Chapter 1: Introduction

Real Estate investing is one of the most simplistic ways to earn money. With a relatively small monetary investment and some sweat equity, you can turn a substantial profit. The future outlook on real estate investing is positive and constantly evolving.

For new investors, one of the most difficult hurdles to overcome is learning the ropes of the real estate business. Real estate transactions are complicated, and if you are not educated on the ins and outs of the business, you potentially could lose large amounts of money, fast.

Before you get started in real estate investing, spend some time thinking about the best approach for your financial situation, personality, and risk tolerance.

One in four residential homes is bought as investment property. Many real estate investors are regular people just like you who make impressive side incomes. Some people even earn enough to make real estate investing their primary income.

In this book, you'll learn about strategies you can use when investing in real estate, the nuances of the complicated sales process, and other points to consider – like real estate law, tax implications, and non-traditional real estate investment options. While being a real estate investor is, at times, stressful, it also can be mentally and financially rewarding.

Chapter 2: Tenderfoot Education in Real Estate Investing

Back in the days of the wild, Wild West, when easterners traveled across this vast country looking for opportunity in the newly opened territories, they were often referred to as a 'tenderfoot'.

This wasn't a complimentary term but it was a rather apt one. The easterners wore 'city' shoes that weren't designed to withstand the rigors of the western terrain. Their hats didn't have wide brims to protect them from the sun and their clothing wasn't made of tough material like denim.

These new westerners didn't know how to take care of themselves and because they didn't know where and what the dangers were they didn't have any idea how to avoid them. If you are just beginning to consider the idea of investing in real estate you are a tenderfoot and you do need some instruction to avoid losing your shirt…and probably your pants, hat and boots, as well.

First you will need to determine what your strategy will be in real estate investing. Do you want to buy a property, fix it up and sell it quickly or do you want to buy a property, hold it and wait for the market to increase? Do you want to deal with renters? All of these questions are ones that you need to answer before you invest in any piece of real estate.

You will need to learn how to investigate the value of properties yourself. It isn't fair to use the time of a real estate agent and have them show you property after property while you try to look for a good real estate investment.

There are several online sites that are helpful in determining the real value of real estate. DO NOT rely on tax values. They are not reliable and they are not accurate either. You can find a real estate agent that you can work with and you can find recommendations for such agents online.

After you have learned how to determine property values yourself and have chosen a real estate agent that you can work with, the next thing that you need is a good broker that you can also work with. Ask your real estate agent for the names of three mortgage brokers.

Then you will need to find out what interest rates and closing costs each one charges. (Check out your local bank or credit union as well). Take copies of your three credit reports and choose a sample property for each broker to run hard numbers on.

Now you are ready to actually make your first investment. You want to choose the lowest price house in the best possible neighborhood to put a contract on.

Let's say the cheapest two-bedroom house in the best neighborhood in Detroit costs $30,000 and the next cheapest, comparable home is listed for $50,000. If you buy the home that is priced at $30,000, you can raise your price to $40,000 the next day and make a dandy little profit.

Now let's talk about closing the deal. First show the seller your pre-qualification letter from your lender. Then get the required inspections for termites and get your appraisal. Once you have all of your 'ducks in a row' so to speak, it takes about 30 days to make the final close.

A note here about any renovations or repairs that you might want to make to the property: Before you close, you might want to think about a Purchase and Renovate loan. A Purchase and Renovate loan wraps the cost of construction up in the loan so you don't have many out-of-pocket expenses. This may require an estimate from a general contractor and plans from an architect as well.

Okay, now let's go back to the first thing that you needed to do and that was to determine your strategy. Now is the time for you to execute that strategy that you have used to invest in this real estate. If you bought it with the strategy of flipping it when the market went up then you just simply wait.

If you bought it with the strategy of renovating and then selling then it is time to start your renovations. On the other hand, if you bought it with the strategy of renting it, it is time to start looking for tenants.

You see, the point of having a strategy for profiting from the purchase of any piece of real estate must be your first decision because everything that comes after that is dependent upon it.

Chapter 3: Strategies in Real Estate Investing

Is Real Estate Investing for You?

Real estate is an intricate business that involves many different legal, financial, and interpersonal aspects. Are you ready to jump into this complicated business? Think about these essential questions before you make your first move.

1. How much money can you invest?

Investing in the real estate market requires capital. The initial outlay of cash needed upfront to acquire a property may be large or small. However, once you assume ownership of the property, you are legally responsible for the full loan amount. Be sure you can afford to invest by looking closely at your personal financial situation. How much cash do you have? What amount of debt and how much interest can your finances handle? Think about how much you can lose.

2. Are you risk tolerant?

Risk and capital go hand-in-hand. How much risk are you comfortable taking on? A large loss to a small investor has a much larger impact than the same amount to a wealthy investor with deep pockets. While risk-taking can be exhilarating, be honest about your finances and think about the level of risk that will be comfortable to you. Do you naturally enjoy taking chances, or do you tend to be more risk adverse? It's essential to success to know your comfort zone.

3. What are your future financial plans?

Are you interested in investing to maintain capital or to get the highest return in the shortest amount of time? Consider the amount of time, money, and risk associated with each scenario. Be logical. A straight 15% profit over a couple of weeks is not realistic. If you are interested in a high return, this usually means there's a longer time commitment, which means your money will be tied up. The value of property can change quickly, leaving you in a higher risk situation.

4. Do you have what it takes?

To be successful in real estate investing, you need to be detail oriented, a quick learner, and have excellent interpersonal skills. You need to have the self-management skills required to determine what you need to know, then go out and learn it and apply it.

5. How much time can you spend?

Think carefully about how much time you can commit to the day-to-day tasks required to be successful in this business. In the beginning, you'll need to spend a lot of time researching and learning about the business. With every endeavor you'll need to spend time working on legal issues, zoning and town issues, insurance, tax concerns, contracts, market research, financing.

If after considering these questions you are still interested in real estate investment – congratulations! This field is one of the most exhilarating ways to make a living.

Your First Real Estate Investment Making your first real estate transaction, either as your primary residence or as a planned investment, can be profitable and exciting, but it can be overwhelming too. Follow these steps when starting out in real estate investing.

1. Educate yourself. This doesn't mean that you need to go back to school, but you do need to take responsibility for what you need to know, and learn it. Study the market you're interested in entering. Use the internet, local land records, and area real estate agents to find the sales prices of comparable properties. Learn about the transaction process, each person's role and responsibility, the legal requirements, and insurance. Each component carries fees that vary, and by researching prices you can avoid losing money.

2. Get your financing in order. A common mistake made by first time investors is to find the property first, then get financing. Before you go out to find that hidden gem, get pre-approved for financing. Decide on a lender by choosing a bank, mortgage company or online loan company.

When talking with your lender, tell them how much you are looking to invest. They'll gather lots of financial information about your income, credit history, liabilities and give you an idea of how much they'll finance.

With the many different financing choices available today, you'll need to decide which option works best for you. Financing plans have different variables including different rates, initial cash investment, and tax implications.

3. Look for your property. Finding real estate that you can make a profit with can be tricky. Use the internet and local newspaper's "Real Estate" section. Look for abandoned and "For Rent" homes. Drive around the area you're interested in and try to find "For Sale by Owner" properties.

4. Negotiate a fair deal. Once you've found the perfect house, you'll need to negotiate for the best price. Don't expect that you'll get a steal. Sellers are trying to the most money for their property, and buyers are trying to pay the least amount. Negotiating well involves working together with the seller to find a win-win situation. Be assertive, but plan to make concessions. Inflexibility often causes expensive delays and added stress.

Profiting in Real Estate

One report indicates that over 59% of total home sales in 2010 were bought as investment properties. This is not a surprise, since home prices have had a high percentage reduction in recent years and the market has been experiencing high returns.

There are many ways to make money investing in real estate. "Flipping" a property means that you buy it, fix it up quickly, and resell it for a profit.

Foreclosures are another way to get investment property, which is when a home owner defaults on a loan and the mortgage holder then puts it up for auction.

With abandon property, it's often unclear who holds the title to the property, so there's extensive title research and legal work that occurs with these properties.

Paper investments, or non-property real estate investments, are when you invest in a mutual funds or bond that is directly related to the real estate market, but not actual property. These investments should be made with advice of a professional broker.

Manage Your Exposure

Managing the risk associated with investing in real estate is key to protecting yourself from loss. The most important aspect of risk management in real estate is to know the law. It's essential that you have a working knowledge of the real estate legal structure and requirements.

After you've researched property availability, cost, and buyer interest, you'll need to hypothesize about what the future holds for your market. Will prices go up or down?

When considering your risk, keep the following points in mind:

1. Think about the local economy. Are there jobs available or are most companies in the area losing jobs? Are new homes being built more or less than over the past 5 years?

2. Make wise financing choices. When picking your funding source, think about how long you plan to keep the property. Adjustable Rate Mortgages (ARMs) are attractive because of their lower down payments and lower rates. You can pick the duration of the loan; typically either 1, 5, or 7 year ARMs and your rate will be adjusted to the prevailing rates after this period of time. If you plan to hold onto a property longer than the ARM, ARMs can cost you more because of the higher interest rates. It may be more prudent to opt for a fixed rate mortgage with the shortest length you can handle financially.

3. Pay a large down payment to reduce your risk. If you can put down 10%, you'll have instant equity in the property, and most likely get a better interest rate.

4. Be creative with your mortgage payments. Make larger monthly payments than require, or make one extra payment a year you'll reduce your principle.

Getting the Highest Return

To make the most money possible in real estate, the standard philosophy is to "buy low, sell high". Most people try to do this, and many do not succeed because it's hard to do. When trying to get the highest return possible, keep your costs down and do everything possible to draw in the highest bidders.

Once you own the property, do as much of the repair work yourself, as long as it is of a professional level. Shoddy work and inferior materials will cost more to correct later. With difficult projects, hire a trained professional from a small scale operation. Large contractors with several employees have to factor their large overhead into their prices.

When looking to maximize your profits, try to save money with your lender. Look around for cheaper loans with the less popular lenders. The large banks and financing companies usually have high fees and rates. Don't accept overpriced fees. For example, your lender is charging $75 to deliver a few papers a short distance, ask for it to be reduced.

By educating yourself on the legal and accounting aspects of real estate transactions, you can save yourself thousands of dollars. If you learn the basics of these two areas you will know when to ask for a professional's help.

When negotiating, be firm but flexible. Attempt to find a win-win situation where both you and the other party walk away from the table happy. Be clear on what you want, and what you can be flexible on. If the other party walks away angry and feeling cheated, they might try to sabotage your attempt to make a profit.

If you are selling your property, it's important to also shop around and negotiate for the best prices on high priced items, real estate commissions, and closing costs.

"Staging" is setting the scene by making your property look its best. You will get the highest price for a property that has been properly prepared.

Actively market your property and you'll get the largest pool of potential buyers possible. It is a benefit to the seller if there are several interested parties in your property.

Buy and Sell at the Right Time

Timing is important in all investments, but unlike other investments bonds, stocks, and mutual funds to name a few; there are two characteristics specific to real estate investing.

1. Real estate transactions take a long time.

2. Each piece of real estate is unique.

In order to buy or sell property it takes a long time, and while the transaction is taking place, the market is constantly changing. This makes timing the purchase or sale of real estate tricky. When you are investing in real estate, you are trying to sell high and then jump back into the market by buying low. Timing the market in such a way is a challenge.

Look for property that is a "fixer upper" to get a good deal. If you have an aptitude for home repair or you know an inexpensive worker, you can increase the value of a home by over 10%.

Search for foreclosure auctions and Notice of Default alerts in the area newspapers and online. Find a good deal on property by anticipating positive change in depressed areas. Up-and-coming neighborhoods, in areas where people have been leaving tend to have lower prices. Find areas where the government is involved in development efforts.

The key to employing any of these strategies is the access to capital. This doesn't mean having an account with a large sum of money in it. Instead, you need to have access to money. By maintaining a high credit score, nurturing an efficient relationship with your lender for quick approval for financing, and having access to liquid assets, you'll be prepared to jump when the right deal comes along.

Even in a slow market, the chance to make a profit investing in real estate is still likely. To do this, however, you'll need to do your homework, have a long-term outlook, and be able to walk away from any deal.

Saving Cash on Little Things Adds Up

Buying property is one of the largest purchases you'll ever make. Even if you aren't putting up a large down payment, by having a mortgage you are making yourself responsible for a sizable amount of money. There's also the possibility of tax consequences.

By saving as much cash as you can, you'll have money for the things that inevitably pop up. As it is, you know you'll need to pay for the closing costs and the initial down payment. Closing costs include the mortgage, fire and hazard insurance, title fees, and many other costly items.

Follow these tips to save money:

1. Get the best financing deal you can find. First and foremost, be sure to have your financing in place BEFORE you make an offer. To get the best deal, research the rates available for your credit score and try to get financing companies to compete for your business. Ask what options are available given your credit rating. Negotiate with your lender to lower or eliminate costly fees and charges. Avoid paying an application fee if you can.

2. Find your own providers. You don't have to use the companies that your agent or lender recommend. This is important when selecting your title and insurance company. Your agent and lender have lists of recommended companies because they have pre-established relationships. Keep in mind that you are the one paying them. Carefully review their fees and

rates before making a decision. You can use any company you wish.

3. Be willing to negotiate. Even a seller in a seller's market needs to be flexible. People sell for many reasons; death in the family, divorce, job transfers, etc. Sellers in these situations are highly motivated to complete the real estate transaction quickly at almost any cost. If you're willing to work with them and be flexible, you may get a good deal.

TIP:

Consider negotiating a deal where the seller pays a larger portion, or all, of the closing costs.

Chapter 4: The Real Estate Sales Process

All About Flipping

Buying real estate and selling it again fast, and ideally for a profit, is called "flipping". This type of real estate investing is completely legal and ethical.

Negative press over flipping real estate probably comes from media coverage of real estate fraud situations, where people have intentionally overpriced the market value of a home, fraudulently completed documents, or worked with others to take advantage of a buyer. None of this happens in an honest flip.

Finding a property that is a good flip requires a few ambitious steps on your part. You'll be looking, most likely, for an under priced home in need of repair. Or you will be looking for a seller that wants to sell fast, thus getting you a lower price.

One way to find property leads is to talk to friends, family, business associates, real estate agents, or bankers. Go out to the neighborhood you're considering and look for "For Sale by Owner" signs, or ring doorbells to see if anyone in the area is considering selling.

Check the public land records and look for "fire sales". This usually means that the owner of the property is having difficulty making mortgage payments. If you contact them and they agree to sell, you're helping them out of their difficult financial situation. And you're getting a property that may make a profit. If done respectfully, there's nothing unethical about this transaction.

TIP:

Make money without even having to find financing. If you enter into a contract to purchase real estate, and then sell the contract to another buyer before the close of escrow, you can turn up to $5000 in profit!

To be a successful real estate flipper, you will need to hone or develop many skills. You will need to have an eye for the diamond in the rough. You should be able to accurately size up buyers. It is best if you are handy and can take care of basic home repairs. It is very important that you are detail oriented and a multi tasking project manager. Flipping involves many details, and it's important to be on schedule with the project to avoid costly delays. Lastly, you will need to have superior interpersonal skills.

Plan to retain the services of a professional accountant, unless you are sufficient at these skills. Also find a good lawyer who can provide you with legal counsel.

Finding Financing – Creative Ideas

For many years, the way to finance real estate was to make a 20% down payment, and get a loan for the remaining 80%. Of course you could make a higher down payment, but 20% was typically the minimum. Luckily, this standard is changing.

There are now several finance options available to the real estate investor. One popular way to finance your purchase is to have a second mortgage. The buyer makes a 5% down payment, and borrows the remaining 15%, usually at a higher interest rate, on a different loan.

Even though it's nice to invest less on a property, the higher interest rate isn't the only drawback. Usually, if the buyer does not meet the 20% minimum, they are required to get costly private mortgage insurance (PMI).

You are able to remove PMI when the loan-to-value (LTV) ratio reaches 80%. This is achieved by paying down the second mortgage and appreciation of the property value. This does not happen often because the property is usually sold or the buyer refinances before PMI can be removed.

For creative investors, other financing sources exist. Manufacturers of homes in planned developments are often willing to provide financing to early buyers.

Another risky and rather complicated way of financing a property is called 'sub2' which stands for 'subject-to'. This type of deal is when the seller gives you the deed to the property, the loan stays in place, but the buyer never legally takes over the loan, just the payments. There are many different versions of this kind of transaction. Because of the complexity and risk, this method of funding an investment is not recommended for beginners.

You can also consider forming a limited partnership to finance your real estate investment. There are many different arrangements on this method. Some types involve each person in the partnership contributing in a portion of the cost, usually 50% each. However, sometimes the profit is distributed relative to the original amount invested. Another arrangement is that one half of the partnership contributes the capital, and the other half provides the needed services, such as repairs on a home that needs to be fixed. There are many different variations of this method.

Government loans are available to low income investors, or buyers who have served in the military. These programs are usually only available for primary residences.

Did you ever think about buying a home on a credit card? This is another method of financing your real estate purchase, although it's usually not recommended. Obviously, the interest rates on most credit cards are substantially higher than loan rates. Another drawback is that lenders determine your creditworthiness based on your outstanding debt, and if you use credit card cash advances to cover the 5-20% down payment that you need, you'll probably get turned down for a loan. This is also true for money borrowed from friends or family, unless you can show that the money is truly a gift.

The Lender's Perspective on Loaning Money

Lenders are in the business of lending people money because they make carefully calculated decisions based on your risk. They have two expectations; that you will repay them and that they will make a profit. To judge if you are capable of meeting those two criteria, lenders look closely at your current financial position and your historical financial situation.

When judging your financial past, lenders will look at:

1. Credit history. They'll review the size and number of previous loans and the repayment history on those loans. They'll also look at your FICO scores and various other raw data.

2. Income history. What is your profit history on your other investments?

Over what length of time? They'll look at the last three years of income statements and tax returns, your debt, and any legal judgments that may impact your financial standing.

3. Your experience with loans. Basically, the lender wants to know that you are trustworthy and will hold up your end of the loan agreement. This means you need to be reliable and make good business decisions.

4. Current holdings and financial situation. Lenders are most interested in liquidity; your cash flow and income.

When lenders are looking at your ability to make a profit, they'll want to know about your total expenses related to the property. How much will it cost you to take care of the property? What will your insurance rates, taxes, and cost of repairs be? The lender wants to see that you can cover your costs associated with home ownership, as well as their interest charges.

Lenders often want short repayment periods, while it usually more beneficial for the buyer to have longer periods. Longer repayment periods mean that you can avoid origination fees, additional appraisal fees, and other costs. When it comes to loans for investment property, a 20 year fixed rate loan is considered a long loan. Normally this includes a balloon payment five to ten years into the loan.

If your lender tries to push you into a shorter repayment period, you can set up an arrangement that you re-price after five years, instead of having to pay a large amount of cash in one lump sum. A common alternative is the prevailing prime interest rate plus 1%.

Keep in mind that most things in real estate investing are negotiable, and that your lender can be your partner in real estate investing. Developing a positive long-term working relationship with your lender can only help you.

Hunting for Your Hidden Gem

Even in a strong market with the new technology available to give up-to-the-minute assessments of properties, an investor can lose large amounts of money in a short period of time. For the best chance to successful obtain your perfect investment property, consider these suggestions:

1. Take advantage of the internet. You can find a "hidden gem" by searching through the millions of properties listed online, and viewing the property's description, pictures, asking price, and legal information. Usually, the only way to avoid a real estate agent fee is to look for property listed For Sale by Owner, or posted on other free sites.

2. Look into getting your own access to the Multiple Listing Service (MLS). A license is required in some areas, but some places you can buy into the service for a fee.

3. Get out and investigate the area that you're considering buying in person. Will the price be held down because of the condition of the neighborhood?

4. If possible, talk to the neighbors. They might give up information about the property that the seller hasn't mention, like the front yard that floods after two days of rain.

5. Get a professional inspection. When you make your offer, add a satisfactory home inspection contingency. Use a trusted professional inspector and carefully review the detailed inspection report. Few properties, even new construction, are perfect. Use the

report to negotiate the repair of problems or an adjustment to the selling price.

The Importance of the Home Inspection

The condition of real estate is different in every situation. To protect yourself when making such a substantial investment, it is important to have a thorough inspection by a trained professional. Make your offer to purchase property contingent on a satisfactory home inspection, and you will avoid investing in a money pit.

What exactly is considered "satisfactory"? Any home containing wood should have a pest inspection, where the inspector looks for evidence of damage caused by termites, mice, carpenter ants or other pests. This inspection is separate from that done by the home inspector.

Your home inspector should focus on every mechanical and structural aspect of the property. They will look for substantial cracks in the foundation, levelness of the structure, and moisture in the basement. Water penetration is evident when there is mold, mildew or efflorescence; a white powder that shows where water has penetrated. High tech inspectors use lasers to see if the things are level and specialized radon gas meters to determine if there is a radon gas issue.

The structure of the home is closely inspected. Homes rest on top of a foundation. Floors have been installed on top of this foundation, and it needs to be inspected to ensure that proper materials have been used. Next, the walls might have improper framing or possible damage from water. Electrical and plumbing systems lie within the walls, and where possible, these interior systems are inspected for wear, out-of-code construction, and damage. Pipes are inspected for leaks or chemical concerns such as lead or rust. Some home inspectors test the water pressure and flow rate of the house.

The home's electrical system is completely inspected. The inspector looks for uncovered switches or outlets, incorrect wiring, insufficient grounding, faulty circuit breakers, or unsatisfactory GFCI trips.

Once in the attic, the inspector should check for water damage and air leaks. The framing is looked at to ensure that it is strong. The underside of the roof is inspected for a good seal where vent pipes go through the roof.

On the roof, the inspector examines it for holes, loose shingles or tile, poor flashing, or any other concern that might cause the roof to not hold up against the elements.

Heating and air-conditioning systems are inspected for adequate flow, duct leaks, and filter condition. Outdoor faucets are tested to be sure they work and don't leak or have inadequate water flow.

All appliances included with the sale of the house are examined. The hot water heater, stove, wood stoves and any other built-in units are check for proper function and standards compliance.

All of this information is compiled in the comprehensive inspection report that is available to the individual or company that paid for the inspection. Inspections benefit the buyer because they can use issues with the property as bargaining chips during negotiations. The home inspection is also beneficial to the seller because they then get an honest assessment of the condition of their property and can make improvements to some items before putting their home up for sale.

The home inspection is one area where a few hundred dollars spent often saves thousands of dollars during the purchase process.

Minimize your Risk with Insurance

In 2005, the median home price rose almost 15% over the previous year, and even more in some real estate markets. The minimum required FICO (credit score) was lowered, some of the documentation requirements were reduced, and the allowance for debt was increased to 45% of income. It is estimated that 30% of all new mortgages are interest-only mortgages. Almost 35% of home loans are Adjustable Rate Mortgages (ARMs). Starting in June 2004, the Federal Reserve has raised interest rates 11 times.

These stats indicate that there has been incredible growth in the real estate market over recent years. As the home prices have risen, so has the associate risk involved with buying and selling property. Thankfully, every type of risk now has an appropriate insurance. Of them all, the two most popular are title and liability insurance.

Title insurance ensures the coverage of any potential financial loss that is a result of an error in the processing and researching of a property title. Any lapses that might happen during the title search process, prior to closing, are covered. The title company will search a public record database to make sure that the property is able to be sold, meaning it's free of encumbrances. Public records are not always completely accurate, and errors can occur.

Liability insurance covers injuries that happen on, or because of, the property. If someone slips and falls on your property, your liability insurance would provide coverage. The more coverage you have, the more expensive it becomes.

Hazard insurance is available for less likely risks such as hurricanes, flooding, or earthquakes.

You can also get coverage for accidents created by humans. This includes chemical spills, electrical malfunctions, vandalism, theft, etc.

It's best to shop around for favourable rates, and pay close attention to your deductible amount, and any limitations on the policy.

Fixing the Property Reaps Financial Rewards

The best way to increase the likelihood that you'd get top dollar for your property is to fix it up. You do not have to be a trainer plumber or carpenter to make your home more attractive to buyers. With just a few tools and some hard work you can give your property a well-maintained appearance.

It's a good idea to go through the house and make minor repairs before showing it, or putting it on the market. A home inspection will likely be done before the final deal, so if you take the time up front to make the minor repairs, you'll be able to avoid some of the potential buyer's bargaining chips in negotiating a deal. Fix the leaky bathroom faucet and fix broken windows.

Take care of your property's curb appeal.

Maintain the landscaping by trimming the lawn and shrubs, and planting some flowers. The outside of the home is what will draw in prospective buyers, or keep them driving.

Ask your neighbors to clean up their yard; offer to take their trash and junk away for them, ask them to move kid's toys, or offer to mow the lawns next to your property. You could even consider giving a small cash incentive after the successful sale of the home.

Your home should be super clean before you show it. It's usually too expensive to replace all the carpeting in a home, but getting it cleaned is affordable. Place your furniture in ways that mask worn spots. Put down new welcome mats and replace worn area rugs. Wash all the windows until they sparkle. Repair worn conduit, and replace air filters on air-conditioning and heating for a fresh look. Give the walls a fresh coat of paint.

Be sure the work looks professionally done, so that people can see the quality of your property. A well-maintained home usually garners a higher sales price than a home that has been neglected.

Selling it Yourself, or Use an Agent?

Selling your home yourself, also called FSBO or For Sale by Owner, is a realistic option thanks to the internet. People sell their own property without an agent because they avoid costly real estate agent commissions. This commission is typically about 6% of the property sale price. Agents work hard for their commissions, and provide valuable insight into the market and sales process.

They usually have valuable experience selling other properties in the area. If you sell it yourself, you stand to save thousands of dollars, but you are taking on all the work that the real estate agent does. Is selling your property FSBO right for you? Think about these points when making this decision:

1. Pricing it right the first time. To price your property correctly, you need to know the market. A poor pricing decision can cost you; under pricing will result in lost potential earnings, and over pricing will cause the home

to sit on the market while you are paying expensive carrying costs. Home prices vary depending on the square footage, lot size, age, and other factors.

2. Use neighborhood comparables to judge the most appropriate list price.

3. Get the word out. If you sell FSBO, you won't have access to the largest, most valuable marketing tool, the MLS. But thanks to the internet, the MLS isn't the only way to market your home. Put out signs, list it on websites, and place ads in the newspaper to let buyers know about your house.

4. Can you negotiate successfully? Some people are born with this skill, and other have to work at it. If you are not a seasoned real estate negotiator, research the subject and learn enough about it to avoid losing money.

5. Be a fast learner. You'll need to do what an agent does. Learn about the sales process, legal issues, contracts, closing process, insurance, and many other aspects of the selling real estate.

6. Patience is important. Selling FSBO is a lot of work and small details, and you are in charge of managing them in order to get the job done.

Making the decision to do it yourself can be rewarding and save a lot of money, but a half-hearted attempted will most likely be unsuccessful.

Marketing Plan Development and Execution

Like it or not, you usually need to spend time marketing your property in order for it to sell. What is marketing? Marketing is the creation of a strategy used to sell an item. Research, promotion, advertising and sales are all part of marketing.

Research your local market, and the prices at which comparables sell. You'll need to have your finger on the pulse of the market during the entire sales process, which can take months. This is important because you may be in negotiations over a long period of time, and knowing the up-to-the-minute standing of your property will help you make educated negotiation decisions.

Advertising is needed to pull together a large group of interested buyers. By having many parties that want to purchase your property you may be able to create a bidding war which will drive up the sale price. How should you advertise? Use all of your advertising resources, like the newspaper, word-of-mouth, flyers, targeted mailings, special trade booklets, and the internet.

The internet is one of the most effective ways to market. There are many real estate investment websites that allow you to post your property with pictures. A comprehensive marketing campaign includes these online marketing tools. Find a site with good traffic and include flattering photos of the interior and exterior of your property. You can consider adding a virtual tour.

If It's Not Selling Quickly Enough

Real estate markets go through cycles. Depending where in the cycle you are, you may find it easy, or difficult, to sell your investment property. If the market has hit a plateau or gone down, you might have to wait for buyers. This will tie up money and make you have to wait to make a profit, which can be frustrating.

There are a few strategies you can use to get yourself out of this type of situation.

1. If it's your primary residence and you can afford to do so, wait it out. The market typically changes every 1 to 5 years, and you can sell on the next upswing.

2. Look at your property from the point-of-view of the buyer and make all necessary improvements. This will make your property more attractive to buyers. Think of what might be a deterrent and account for it. For example, if you live next to a loud highway, close the windows and play soft music to take away from this drawback.

3. Stage the house. Set out a few bouquets of flowers, turn the lights on, put on some light background music, bake some fresh cookies for a homey smell and welcomed snacks for visitors. Put out a flyer on

the property with plenty of attractive pictures, a reminder of the property highlights and your contact information. Make it so the buyer can see themselves living there. Buyers want a home they that makes them proud.

4. Encourage your neighbors to help you improve the appearance of the neighborhood.

5. Make sure you've priced the home correctly. Markets shift frequently, so you might not be priced competitively priced for the current market.

If you've tried these tips and the property has still not sold, try taking it off the market for awhile, and then list it again after re-checking your pricing. When houses sit on the market too long, potential buyers assume there must be something wrong. Extensively advertise your property. Making the extra effort to get your house sold will only help you make a profit.

Negotiating a Win-Win Deal

When negotiating, arm yourself with information and knowledge and you will be well equipped to broker a fair deal. Find out as much as you can about real estate law, the current market, and the other person's situation. If you are buying the house find out why they are selling. Are they in foreclosure? Has something happened personally that makes them eager to get rid of the property at any reasonable price? Find out how long the place has been on the market, the number of other offers, if any, and at what amount. Is there outstanding debt on the home, and if so how much? Are they up-to-date with their payments?

Most sellers won't just give out this information. Try to determine their status by giving up a bit of your own information first. Be careful about what you say because the seller might be able to use it when negotiating with you later.

When you are engaged with the other party in negotiating a contract, you're trying to come to a mutual agreement on the price of the property and terms. Consider the area comps, true condition of the property from the inspection report, and seller's situation. Before getting involved in any negotiation have your financing in place by being pre-approved. Before signing any written offers or contracts, seek legal counsel.

TIP:

Make your offer in a non-round number. An offer of $233,200 vs. $230,000 might catch the seller off guard and leave them curious about what information you have that they don't.

Chapter 5:
Other Considerations in Investing

Know the Real Estate Law

Every part of real estate involves the law. There are many complicated legal pieces and many different people are involved in any real estate transaction.

First and foremost, the contract is most important part of buying and selling property. The primary purpose of a contract is to show mutual assent to the agreement by both parties to the exchange in writing. Verbal agreements are not binding. To be valid a contract, it must include the following:

1. Identification of the parties involved and the agreed upon price
2. Specific "consideration" must be stated; something of value that's being exchanged, usually money
3. Signatures of each party involved

There are checks-and-balances to protect people in every situation and to protect the overall system. Appraisals are used to ensure that the property is worth what the lender and seller have purported. The appraisal prevents shady deals being stuck between investors and mortgage brokers. Commercial property has its own laws regarding use and sale. If there are tenants living in the property, there are specific laws to protect the landlord and tenants. Lenders are held to the law by how much they can loan, what documents and insurance are required, and even how they market their financing programs.

It's important to know about tax law, or get advice from a professional, since it greatly impacts your success in real estate investing. Mistakes are costly, and by protecting yourself you can make decisions that will help your bottom line rather than take away your profits.

Investing Tax Implications

Before covering the subject of real estate tax law, understand that the following should not be thought of as legal advice. Seek legal advice from your attorney or accountant when making any legal or tax decisions.

Each area has its own tax codes, but here are a few general tips to consider that apply in most locations:

1. You can sell your primary residence tax-free if you've lived there for two or more years. Investment property that's been sold is subject to capital gains tax, and if held for less than one year, it's at the regular income tax rates which can be as high as 35%. If the property is held one year or more before selling, it's considered a long term capital gain and is typically taxed at 15%.
2. You can also sell tax-free if you keep the property as a residence for 730 days, not necessarily in a row. If you sell and reinvest

the cash into a home of equal or greater value, you won't need to pay tax.

3. "Like kind" investment trades, also known as the 1031 exchange, can be used to defer taxes. You can use this to trade undeveloped land for property with a house, a rental home for a commercial building, etc. You can take 45 days to locate up to 3 substitute properties, and you must have the closing within 180 days. You also need to retain a facilitator, or neutral party, to keep accurate records and hold the money. You cannot do a 1031 exchange with your primary residence.

4. Mortgage interest can be deducted from your taxes. Loans valued at up to $1 million are eligible, and origination fees and points can be included.

Since the tax law is so complicated, it's best to seek professional assistance anytime you are in a situation that's out of the ordinary. The amount you pay for their services will be saved tenfold by their expertise in the field.

The Pros and Cons of Rural vs. Urban Investments

One real estate trend is the shift of buyers from populated urban locations to less populated rural places. Unique properties like vineyards, Bed & Breakfasts, horse farms, and agricultural farms, have realized increased property values thanks in part to aging, financially secure, baby boomers. Although these locations are desirable when investing in real estate, there are some challenges associated with rural properties.

Finding a property can be a challenge. With the increased popularity of people working from home, and more retirees looking for rural retreats, it can be difficult to find an investment property at a bargain price.

Finding reliable and qualified contractors that are affordable often presents a challenge in rural locations. You may need to pay a premium for skilled labor, even if the average income in the area is lower than in the city.

When property is unique, it's difficult to appraise. Many rural properties don't have realistic comps, so the value is essentially guessed. Lenders are aware of this type of situation, so they might to be less willing to finance a loan for a one of-a-kind property. This usually isn't a problem if the buyer has solid credit and can provide a more substantial down payment.

When it comes time to sell a rural investment property, you will need to market your property over a larger area to pull together a group of interested, and qualified, potential buyers.

Investing in Real Estate Foreclosures

While some foreclosures may look appealing to the real estate investor, it's essential to consider many factors before you enter into a deal involving a foreclosed property.

What is foreclosure? It's a legal process that occurs when a mortgage holder takes back a property when payments are not current.

By buying a foreclosed property, you are entering into a legal mess. Some foreclosure situations allow for the 'right of redemption'. This means that the property owner can make back payments and take back the title. Obviously, you want to stay away from this. When considering a foreclosure, look for situations where, at minimum, a Notice of Default has been given.

A unique point about foreclosures is that the property is sold "as is". There are no warranties and no title insurance. Have a professional inspection beforehand, and never make an offer without looking at the property personally. If there are problems with the property but you are looking for a house to fix, reduce your offer appropriately. Before buying, conduct a thorough title search.

Two other types of foreclosure are REO and 'short sale' deals. REO stands for "real estate owned". This is when the lender owns the property because it was auctioned, but no one bought it. You can find a REO bargain, but be very careful. The property usually wasn't bought for a reason. Short sale deals happen when a lender will take less money than remains on the existing loan.

Investing in Commercial Property

Commercial real estate investment (CREI) accounts for a fraction of all real estate investments, with residential property being the largest segment. Just because it is a small piece of the pie doesn't mean it's less complicated.

Commercial property is most often bought for business purposes as an investment. Even if it's an apartment building with several apartments, it's considered commercial.

When investing in commercial property, you have to invest more money, which requires excellent credit. By putting more money down, you have exposed yourself to greater risk. Commercial investors also need to determine their capitalization rate (cap rate) and Gross Rent Multiplier (GRM) to decide if an investment is a good decision.

The cap rate and GRM are useful calculations when investing. The cap rate formula is: Annual Net Operating Income/Purchase Price. Usually, a sound investment has an 8-10% cap rate. The lower the percentage, the higher the risk and the lower the anticipated profit. The formula used to calculate the GRM is: Purchase Price/Monthly Gross Operating Income.

You should also consider the property comps, appraisal vs. assessment, income and replacement costs when considering if a deal is worth it.

Commercial properties are also tricky because the economic conditions of an area often dictate the occupancy of commercial property.

When buying commercial property, you'll need to first educate yourself on area zoning, leasing rules, commercial law, building maintenance, and other legal issues. Since the property will most likely be rented, you'll need to consider fire safety, internet and telephone capabilities, more complex plumbing and electrical needs, security systems, and more. Only when a landlord has a triple-net lease; where the tenant pays for and coordinates all maintenance, repairs, and insurance will the involvement be less.

Of course a profit can be made from CREI. Although there are more risks, the potential profit is often higher.

The Pros and Cons of Renting Property

Sometimes investors hold onto property with the hopes of making a profit through rental, while benefiting from the capital appreciation and beneficial tax code.

When deciding whether to hold or sell a property, calculate out your estimated taxes if you keep the property, versus selling it. Hypothesize about future sales prices are going based on interest rates, trends, and the current market.

If you've decided to become a landlord, keep the following in mind:

1. Have all applicants complete an application. Use this information to conduct a complete background check; review rental and credit history, and talk to their references, previous landlords and employers.

2. Use a contract that's easy to understand and is fair. It should include information about the amount and stipulations of the deposit, under what conditions and how much notice is needed for the landlord to enter the rental, who is responsible for what, etc.

3. Do what you say, and more. Keep your tenants happy and chances are they'll pay the rent. If you're slow to respond to maintenance requests or don't keep up the property, they might stop paying rent.

4. If a tenant is late with the rent, find out why right away. Encourage them to have the rent paid by the due date by reminding them of the late fee clause in the lease. Keep clear records of payments because you may need this information if legal action were ever required.

5. If you do need to take legal action, try to first go through arbitration. Cases are typically handled faster and more efficiently.

Alternative Real Estate Investment Instruments

There are ways to invest in real estate without ever having to deal with the nitty gritty parts of the business; no inspection, appraisal, or marketing. Real Estate Financial Trusts (REITs), Mortgage-Backed Securities (MBS), and Self-Directed IRAs are all ways of investing in real estate on paper alone.

Real Estate Financial Trusts (REITs) are mutual funds that focus on real estate; investments are made in both physical property and mortgage portfolios. It's handled like other securities and has special tax situations. REITs often have better yields and provide easier access to cash than traditional property investment.

There are Mortgage, Equity, and Hybrid REITs. Mortgage REITs invest in mortgages, with revenue coming from the mortgage interest. Equity REITs own and invest in actual real estate, with most of the revenue coming from rental income. Hybrid REITs are a combination of both.

Just like other mutual funds, once purchased they can't be cashed in through the fund, but have to be sold to another investor through a broker.

REITs can be considered high yield, since dividends are paid out to shareholders at 90% or more of taxable earnings. Dividends plus appreciation equals the total return, and REITs are comparable to small-cap stock in that about 66% of the return comes from the dividends. As a result, REITs are impacted by changes in interest rates. When interest rates increase, the price of REITs usually decline.

Mortgage-Back Securities are bonds backed by a group of mortgage loans. Just like other type of bonds, you earn a coupon rate of interest. Unlike other bonds, however, investors get repayments of the principle in small parts, over the duration of the MBS, as the mortgage loans that back the MBS are paid off, instead of in one lump sum when the security matures.

One of the reasons that the MBS is a stable investment is because there are so many loans in the pool; the few loans that default or pay off early do not eliminate the investor's profit.

When choosing between closed MBS and pre-payable MBS, determine if interest rates are likely to rise or fall. Mortgage holders can pre-pay their mortgages, and if interest rates drop people will refinance to take advantage of better rates, both scenarios will negatively impact the MBS investor. If interest rates are expected to drop, a closed MBS is the better option.

A Self-Directed Individual Retirement Account

(IRA) can hold assets such as land, single family residences, and commercial property instead of just cash. Before you invest in any real estate investment, contact a financial professional and do your own research to make the best decision for you.

Real estate is a multi-faceted, multi-billion dollar industry. As an investor, it's important to know the business and take some calculated risks in order to turn a profit. From each investment experience you will gain valuable skills that you can apply to future investing endeavours.

Chapter 6: Why Invest in Urban Real Estate?

Most investors are not interested in investing in urban real estate. This means that there is a wide open opportunity for those who ARE interested in investing in urban real estate. You will likely hear umpteen reasons why you should NOT invest in urban real estate so let me give you a few good reasons why you SHOULD invest in urban real estate.

First let's discuss the pricing of urban real estate. If you keep your 'ear to the ground' so to speak you can find some real hidden gems in the urban real estate market. Not every low price is a good deal, of course, and just like with every real estate investment that you ever make, you should be certain that you do your homework.

Really great deals turn up in every real estate market for one reason or another. Don't miss those terrific investment opportunities simply because the property is in an urban area.

Then there are the Section 8 tenants to be considered. Here is an obvious advantage to investing in urban properties. Government subsidized housing is a 21st century reality and under Section 8 the government pays a full 80% of the monthly rent. These renters are often referred to as 'Section 8 tenants'. There is, of course, always a waiting list of potential renters and they all want to move into YOUR urban investment property.

That adds up to a very nice and sure monthly income for you. Renters don't always pay their rent but the government does send checks on time and in full thus eliminating much of the rent collection hassle.

Let's not overlook the fix and flip opportunity afforded by urban real estate investments. Okay, let's face it. Today's real estate market could be better....a lot better...but just because the over-all market doesn't seem to be all that healthy at the moment that doesn't mean that there aren't some great fix and flip opportunities out there and particularly in the urban areas. The trick to making a profit on an urban property is to sell with incentives included and, if it is a rental property, with a tenant already in residence.

Don't forget about the good old government of the United States of America. The government funds projects to rehab entire neighborhoods in urban areas and they do soon a regular basis. The local government gets funding and usually offers attractive incentives to developers and home owners investing in these urban neighborhoods.

Not only that but you can negotiate some really astounding interest rate offers that will let you keep your money in your pocket and out of and danger at all. This creates a win/win/win situation. The government gets to spend money which they seem to do so well. The inhabitants of the neighborhood get better housing and you make a nice profit. Everybody wins!

There is the tired old real estate saying, "The only three things that matter in real estate are location, location and location." That really is NOT necessarily true. Do you remember playing the board game Monopoly when you were a kid? Remember those first little properties that were located right at the beginning of the game?

They were cheap. They were REALLY cheap. If you bought one of those rights at the beginning of the game, so to speak, you could have a hotel up on it almost immediately and every player in the game was going to have to land on it and pay you. It was a pretty good location but not an expensive one. It was one that you could afford to make improvements on quickly.

Remember? Think of investing in urban real estate like you would think of investing in Baltic Avenue or Mediterranean Avenue. You don't pay much for the property but improvements don't cost much either and you can make a profit easily and quickly. It was good strategy for Monopoly and it is a good strategy for real live urban real estate investing.

Urban property investments meet all of the criteria for sound real estate investing.

There is a good rental market in an urban area. There are lots of people who need housing and that housing is very often government subsidized.

Urban property is usually low priced and can even be purchased at extremely attractive interest rates as well.

The market is stable in urban neighborhoods. There isn't a boom or bust mentality. Demand is not likely to decrease.

Investing in urban property can be a very good decision but you should always do your homework before you invest.

Chapter 7: The Secret to Real Estate Riches Lies in Location, Location, and Location

According to the old real estate saying, "The only three things that matter in real estate are location, location and location." The fact is that a ten bedroom, eight bath home with cathedral ceilings and a swimming pool that is sitting next to a garbage dump is nearly worthless.

On the other hand a little one bedroom, one bath shack sitting in the middle of downtown Dallas would be worth a small fortune. So you can see that the location is of the utmost importance when you are considering a piece of real estate to invest in.

What is it that makes the location of a piece of real estate valuable? The answer is fairly simply really. The value is based on nothing more than the desirability factor. Desirability is a fluctuating intangible that is really hard to nail down.

Property that is totally undesirable to one person might be just the next person's dream come-true. And this phenomenon is true for real estate investors and for home buyers and for renters. It is true for all aspects of the real estate market.

The main point for any real estate investor to consider first is what their strategy will be for making a profit on a property. Buying is only half of the equation and whether the location of the property is good or bad depends upon that profit strategy.

For example: If an investor is going to invest in a property with the intention of just waiting for the market to go up, prime real estate is probably the very best choice. Locations that are near entertainment centers or developing areas would be best because the likely hood that the property will increase in value simply by waiting is a pretty good bet.

On the other hand, if an investor is going to invest in a property with the intention of renting it and making a monthly income from it, he might be better off to look into urban properties. Urban properties wouldn't be considered 'prime' real estate but they are 'prime' rental properties.

Then there are real estate investors who are handy with their hands. They can make repairs and renovations to rundown properties themselves, sell it for a great deal more than their purchase price and make a very nice profit. The location that these kinds of real estate investors often find the best is in neighbourhoods that are made up of mid priced homes in working neighbourhoods.

There are many factors that real estate investors consider when they are deciding which property to invest in. One factor can be what I call the 'snob' factor.

It's strange but people will pay a lot more money for a small property in the 'right' neighbourhood than they will for a larger property in a less desirable neighbourhood. However...one person's definition of a 'good' neighbourhood will not be anywhere close to another person's definition of a 'good neighborhood.

Then there is the 'visibility' factor. If a neighbourhood or an area has become famous or even infamous, property values rise regardless of the location. Convenience is another factor when considering the desirability of the location of a piece of property. People do like to live close to where they work and where their children attend school. Rising gas prices just might work wonders for real estate prices in inner cities.

The desirability of the location of any piece of real estate can be determined by a great many different factors for real estate investors and for home buyers and renters. If the location is desirable for the investor's purposes he will invest.

If the location is desirable for a home buyer's purposes then he will buy. If the location is desirable for a renter's purposes then he will rent. So basically, you can roll all of the various factors for determining whether a location is good or bad into one simple work; desirability.

We are a nation of individuals. We all see things from a different point of view. Look around. There are people living everywhere. They live in big cities, small towns and in urban and rural areas. Who can determine what a 'good' location really is?

There is a proverb that says, "Beauty is in the eye of the beholder". The modern version would be 'whatever floats your boat is good'. In real estate it would translate to 'if the location serves your purpose then it's a good location'.

Chapter 8: How to Find Hot Markets for Buying Investment Property

Investing in real estate is not a new path to financial success. It is a well worn path and it is so well worn because it is such an effective way to make a great deal of money in a relatively short period of time. But you have to be a forward thinker to make any serious money in the buying and selling of real estate.

The objective is to buy low and sell high and that means that you have to make a guess (an EDUCATED guess) as to what is GOING to happen tomorrow or next week or next year or ten years from now and not base your decisions on what happened yesterday, or last week, or last year or ten years ago.

Think about the neighbourhood that you grew up in. Your mom and dad bought the house when the subdivision was new. It isn't new anymore. It isn't on its way UP. It is on its way DOWN.

The residents and the buildings are all beginning to show their age. That is the nature of real estate. What goes up will eventually go down. You always want to buy when the area is on the rise and not when it is in decline. There are, of course, exceptions to this rule but there aren't many.

In short; you need to find the hot markets when buying investment property and in a nutshell the hot market is where the people are GOING. Determining where people are going is the trick.

Buying in an area that is already popular can be a hot market providing you can make a good deal on the property but finding out about upcoming changes in the infrastructure can lead you to where people will be going in the future.

Infrastructure changes are such things as major highway construction, marinas or entertainment facilities. Basically, you base your real estate market investments upon the cold hard facts and not what you hope will happen or what your barber tells you.

Right now is the time to invest in real estate in the USA. Real estate investing is not an exact science. You always have to weigh the risk against the potential reward and if you do decide to invest in overseas property it is wise to employ a local attorney to oversee the process.

Then there is always the 'cool' factor that shouldn't be overlooked when searching for hot investment real estate. For example: in Detroit, due to the fact that the auto industry will re-emerge. Suddenly, Detroit will become a very 'cool' place to live and real estate prices will soar! So don't overlook 'cool'.

Keep both eyes on large corporation expansion plans. When corporations build, expand or even relocate the real estate market will boom simply because of demand for housing and small businesses. If a Wal-Mart is going to be built in a town, can a McDonald's be far behind? And all of those people who will be coming in to run Wal-Mart and all of the small businesses that it spawns will need housing.

Yes! Business can cause real estate prices to go up and can create hot properties for investment purposes! Remember that old song that Willie Nelson recorded, "You have to know when to hold 'em, know when to fold 'em, know when to walk away and know when to run". Although the song was about gambling the advice is solid for investing in real estate.

Choosing what properties to invest in should be made strictly upon solid facts. A building permit for a marina is solid proof that a marina is going to be built and that the adjacent property values are going to go up.

Your cousin telling you that he HEARD that a marina was going to be built is NOT a fact. Its hearsay and you shouldn't bet a lot on hearsay! Investing in real estate is an excellent way to get a very high return but you really do need to know what you are doing to keep from losing your shirt.

Chapter 9: 101 Tips for Selling Real Estate

So….you'd like to sell your house? Great! Everyone's doing it. But this is your first time and you'll be doing the sale yourself. Nervous? Of course!

The fact is, it's only unnerving because you haven't got a clue about the dynamics of selling a house, or your house. It's the one asset you have where you've plunked down your lifetime savings. Now you want it all back!

That equity you were slowly building over these years will come back to you a hundredfold because you've thought about it long enough to realize that there is a handsome profit waiting to be made.

Don't worry! This episode in your life doesn't need to be a drama of horrors. In this book, I have collected important tips for you the first timer; all 101 of them, in fact.

And when that check finally lands on your hands and the last box has been shipped out of your house to make way for the new owners, it will be exhilarating, more exhilarating than you've ever imagined it to be.

Study the tips. Some you already know, no doubt. But even with 101 or 1001 tips, you'd still need professional advice – you managed to eliminate the real estate agent, but you'll still need your lawyer (or notary) and your accountant.

You need to consult with other professionals as well; like the professional house inspector who can dish out valuable advice about repairs and maintenance.

These tips can help you map out a selling strategy for your house, and when you turn the lock for the last time, you'll come out of the experience wiser. And yes, wealthier too.

The confidence you gain by getting your feet wet the first time could – who knows? – make you want to do it the second time, and then a third time…and more!

Chapter 10: Category 1: Knowledge is Power

Tip 1: Before anything else, grab a powerhouse of knowledge.

If you've decided to dispense with a real estate agent to avoid paying those ridiculous commissions, then start thinking like one.

How? Three to six months before your target sale, bone up on home selling strategies. If you have friends or colleagues who've worked in real estate, talk to them, but don't tell them you're thinking of your selling your house so they won't try to convince you to do otherwise.

Ask them about mistakes they've made or mistakes that their relatives and friends have made. Survey the entire landscape. Personal experiences are always an excellent source of knowledge and strategies.

Tip 2: Be a listener, and be a GOOD one

Hold casual conversations with at least 3 real estate agents who work in the area where your house is located. Be attentive to what they say about location. It's helpful to know how much your civic address is worth.

While location is the predominant argument in real estate, this rule may not always apply. Perhaps location is the least of your potential buyer's worries. Don't overlook the fact that buyers have typical and unusual reasons for buying a house. Many have jumped into the arena of investment property.

While most people buy houses so they can live in it, there are those who like to play the market and want to make a killing. Sell your house with an open mind. Don't let the factor of location discourage you, or encourage you too much.

Tip 3: Basic rule: don't get locked out of the market because you've overpriced your house!

Continue building up on that knowledge base: make it a daily habit of reading real estate ads everyday. Get the average selling price of a house identical to yours.

If you have the luxury of time, you may even want to drive around these houses for sale and judge for yourself whether or not the price they're asking is justified.

Some homeowners have illusions as to what their houses cost. Is the price they ask reasonable, or way out of proportion to the looks and location of the property?

Tip 4: What are the ads saying?

Get a feel of how real estate ads are worded.
- What are the key words and phrases?
- What ads caught your attention?

- Why?
- Does the ad sound credible?
- Does the ad provide adequate information to provoke interest, or does it leave the reader indifferent?

Use these ads as a model for your own.

Tip 5: Play detective

Do a bit of detective work: try to keep track of real estate ads that appear only a couple of days (house could have been sold in just a matter of days) and ads that seem to be in the paper forever (why can't the advertiser sell? What's preventing him from selling?) This is where wording might clue you into the reasons.

Tip 6: Read and devour all that you can!

Build up some more on your knowledge power by visiting your local library, and browsing through books and magazines about real estate in general (and selling homes in particular).

Be on the alert for people who've written about their personal experiences in selling their homes. Being well informed is still your best weapon.

Tip 7: Realistically speaking, my house is really worth...

Set realistic goals: if houses like yours in your area are asking for $250,000.00 don't think you could make a lot more just because you have a rose garden and your neighbor doesn't.

Deviating too much from the mainstream can work against you. Don't stop buyers from calling you because your price is way too much the average prices for your area.

Tip 8: Play the real estate game seriously.

Bear in mind that the "no risk, no gain" philosophy may not always work in real estate. Real estate is a smart, serious business. It's better to have brains than guts! Feed your brain with information you will need when you finally do sell your house. Real estate information is not a scarcity.

There are thousands of web sites dedicated to real estate. And the library holds a wealth of information on the subject.

Tip 9: Get only enough to get you started

Too much analysis leads to paralysis. Arm yourself with adequate knowledge and then get moving! Don't let fear or over-confidence immobilize you. If you want to sell your house successfully, fear has no place in the grand scheme of things, nor does arrogance.

Chapter 11 Category 2: Know Thy Area and Community

Tip 10: Good schools? But of course!

Think about what's special about your community, then conjure up an ad that might attract say, a young couple with school-age children. Find out how many private and public schools there are, and how near are they to your house.

Many times, good schools are the deal clinchers. For young families, schools are a top priority. If the schools in your community have won awards from the private and public sector, or if you hear about any achievements, mention them to your buyers.

Tip 11: It's the fitness thing, you know.

Do an inventory of your community's attractions. How many parks, tennis courts are there? Is there a YMCA? All these facilities play a major role in the decision to buy, especially if the husband or wife is a fitness freak.

Tip 12: And what about concerts and that kind of thing?

Don't overlook the entertainment factor: how many restaurants and movie theaters does your area have? What about concert halls and other cultural activities?

Young couples, especially those with no children, like to eat out often.

They also want the assurance that if they don't feel like entertaining friends for dinner at home, they can go for a concert or a show to spend a relaxing weekend. A very cultural community filled with activities is a huge factor, not only for them, but also for their children.

Tip 13: Will I fit in the area?

The ethnic factor: if your area has a strong multi-cultural presence, this might be an attraction for newly arrived immigrants in search of a house. The feeling of wanting to feel "at home" is a strong motivator. You may think it a trivial matter, but buyers do ask if there's a sushi restaurant in the area, or if there are any Jewish Synagogues nearby.

Are there meeting places where members of ethnic communities can mingle and share views, cuisine and stories about "back home"?

Tip 14: Is there a doctor in the house?

Does your area have a good hospital? What makes that hospital a plus factor? Families that have aging in-laws in town would like to know if they can get medical help immediately in case of an emergency.

Also, if your local area hospital is known for a particular specialization make sure you let your buyers know.

Tip 15: How is the transportation system?

How far are the major highways from your house?
Where is the next largest city? How developed is
your area's public transportation system? Proximity
to a subway station is typically seen by many as a
benefit because downtown parking is expensive. This
constitutes a great advantage also for teenaged
children who attend university downtown.

Tip 16: No gossiping allowed!

Are you in friendly terms with your neighbors? If
you're selling a condo or a duplex, the next owners
are usually curious about what kind of neighbors live
in the same enclave.

Show your neighborliness, but don't gossip about the
neighbor on your right. Chances are prospective
buyers are only interested if the neighbors are quiet or
rowdy. They're not interested in your neighbor's
alcohol problem.

Tip 17: Help, my car's been snowed in!

How efficient are your city's services? Does the area
have enough firemen, snow removal trucks, and
garbage collection systems? What about facilities for
recycling waste material?

The more you know about your community's
services, the better you can capitalize on these selling
points.

If either the wife or husband has had a hip fracture, efficient snow clearing by the municipal government is reassuring. Not many cities can say that their snow is cleared on time.

Tip 18: Cavities?

Is the city water fluoridated? You'll be amazed at how some parents make a big deal of this. Studies have revealed that cities where the water has been fluoridated have a lower incidence of tooth decay among school-age children.

Perhaps this looks like a minor detail to you, but remember, the intelligent buyer is taking a thorough inventory of the community and its services.

Chapter 12: Category 3: Know Thy Abode

Tip 19: Getting to know your house...for the last time

Okay, you have a good understanding of real estate, you know your community, and now it's time to know your house like the back of your hand.

Every house has a hidden defect or a very visible fault. Take pencil and paper and do a tour, taking down all the weaknesses that can potentially be spotted by buyers when they visit. Go around your house several times to make sure you've covered everything.

You want to discover the defect before the buyer does. Spare yourself some embarrassment. Don't underestimate the buyer's ability to see through walls!

Tip 20: Did you say an in-ground pool?

If your house comes with a swimming pool, mention it! An in-ground swimming pool adds a lot of value to a house.

Make sure the pool is clean and there are no floating algae or fungi when the buyers come knocking at your door.

If there's anything that can be quite disconcerting it's a pool with no water, dead leaves and little creatures floating about, or large cracks in the pool. A pool isn't fun without a heater. Let your buyer know that the pool's heater is working.

Tip 21: Put romance back in their lives...

If you live in an area with a colder climate; Minnesota for instance, a fireplace makes a good sell, so don't forget to mention it.

This particular detail can go into the ad, or you can surprise your potential buyer when they come to visit. It's all up to you. Find out what the real estate agents say about fireplaces.

In Florida for example, a fireplace is not something you'd think a house should have, but in upscale, gated communities, families do have nice fireplaces in the living room or basement. Ambiance, that's why.

Tip 22: See, this garage door is really simple to operate!

Check your garage door mechanism and see if it's working properly. You'll want to demonstrate to potential buyers that your garage is in tip top shape.

You may also want to show them your maintenance records (garage doors usually need to be inspected and lubricated once every two years, depending on how recent your garage door and mechanism are).

Tip 23: I never promised you a rose garden.

Check your front and back yards. Are they well-kept or do they look like they've been neglected for the last six months? Is your grass healthy and green and well manicured?

When buyers look for a house, they customarily concentrate on making adjustments inside the house; they understand that part of the house buying process is renovation.

At least they're prepared for this event, but when they see that the outside of the house also needs major attention, they could get discouraged, and dismayed no doubt to see such an unkempt front yard and backyard.

Tip 24: You'll have a roof over your head for the next 25 years.

Make a list of major and minor renovations you've undertaken in the last five years. Keep this list in your pocket so that when you give the house tour, you can mention these renovations.

Things like "my wife and I had the roof changed entirely even before the 25-year period. One thing you won't have in this house is a leaking roof".

Or else: "These kitchen cabinets and drawers were given a face lift only three months ago".

Or perhaps: "We decided to install smoked glass in one part of the kitchen to hold our crystal collection". Then turn on the light of the smoke glass cabinet to show some dramatic effect, the expensive crystal collection and the dim lighting.

Tip 25: Wow, a home spa!

Pay attention to the bathrooms. Make sure they have good lighting, squeaky clean faucets and a shiny, sparkling bathtub. A stained bath tub is unsightly.

Hang some of your best linens for the visit. A bathroom that smells and looks clean can be a persuasion point. Count yourself lucky if you have a whirlpool or a large Roman bath.

For couples just recently married, the whirlpool or spa might just bring you closer to finalizing that deal. One thing with house hunters; they start with a budget in mind, but watch how they're easily swayed to stretch that budget a little more when they see amenities that they otherwise would not have thought about previously.

Tip 26: A house that's safe and sound.

Buyers are likely to ask you about insulation and energy efficiency systems in your house. If you don't know or can't remember, be honest and say so.

However, it definitely would be to your advantage if you can speak knowledgeably about the "inner character" of your dwelling. The old installation materials of older houses were declared a health risk by the US and Canadian governments many years ago, and house builders have switched to safer insulation materials.

Make sure you mention this if you do know, especially if you're dealing with a buyer who happens to be a lawyer.

Tip 27: What? No hot water again?

Many people don't know this, but if you were smart enough to have your water heater checked periodically, say so.

Water heaters, in order for them to work efficiently, have to be inspected regularly. Over time, water heaters get an accumulation of chemicals in the bottom. Even if a new roof costs a lot more than a new water heater, buyers appreciate the present owner's thorough "sense of maintenance" by looking into details that homeowners usually overlook.

Tip 28: Someone forgot to look up the ceiling…

One real estate agent in Washington DC remarked that she was approached by a couple to sell one of the "cutest houses in the neighborhood".

It had excellent potential; large backyard, nice French bay windows, a second floor landing area that was large enough to accommodate a family gathering, and solid wooden floors.

The only thing wrong, according to the real estate agent, was the entire lighting system. The lamps and chandeliers looked like they were put there since the time of Adam and
Eve.

She suggested to the present owners to replace all the lights and to invest in good quality lamps. The cutest house in the neighbourhood eventually sold; just three weeks later for $900,000.00

Chapter 13: Category 4: Your Motives for Selling: Watch Out for the Psychological Effect

Tip 29: Why am I selling?

You made the decision of selling the house. You went through the motions of going over your house and looking for things to repair.

Before you get to the next step of advertising your house in the paper and by word of mouth; spend some quiet time to yourself so you can gauge your true feelings about why you want to sell your house.

If you have compelling reasons or circumstances that force you to sell, this may affect your position as a seller. As the property owner, you should always be on the driver's seat.

Only you can dictate the terms of sale. If you're emotionally or financially disadvantaged, you may want to put off selling your house until you're 100% convinced that you're ready emotionally and financially.

Tip 30: Not the time to be fickle...

If your house holds much sentimental value and you feel that parting with it will affect you psychologically, assess how strong your emotional attachment to your house is.

Once the house is sold, there is no turning back. Sale contracts are legally binding. You can't appear at the doorway of the new owners and say, "Sorry, I've changed my mind. I acted irrationally by selling. I want my house back!"

Tip 31: Nostalgia is a strong feeling

You want to sell because you're getting divorced from your husband of 25 years? If you no longer love your husband, but still love your house, think twice about selling.

If the house means that much to you, then perhaps you may want to re-consider. A house is not only a physical structure. It is a refuge, a reservoir of memories of a family that built a future together.

Sell your house if you have to, but if you'll spend sleepless nights regretting the decision to sell, you might be risking your mental health.

Tip 32: I'm in a bind…

Financially strapped? Many people think of selling their house to acquire much-needed cash. Your house is your only asset and perhaps the only asset that banks will look at if you apply for a loan.

Instead of selling, you may consider the option of using the equity you've built up in your home to apply for a loan. But don't sell just because you need cash. Banks are often willing to give you room to maneuver on your house equity.

Tip 33: My home isn't a hotel!

If you hesitate about selling your house because you want your children to have a place to stay when they visit, remember that you raised them to be responsible, self sufficient adults.

If you really want to sell your house, this should be the least of your worries. Your grown children can perfectly manage on their own. Your house isn't the Four Seasons!

Tip 34: Listen up, but stay with your convictions!

Remind yourself that it's your house, so buyers should play by your rules. Don't let some smooth talking buyer convince you that your house isn't worth that much.

You did your homework, so you're the only one who knows what you should be getting for your house. Remember it's the buyer who needs a house, not you. If one buyer is starting to get on your nerves, there are other buyers.

Tip 35: I'm selling, no matter what.

Banish your fears and emotional ups and downs because they only lead to inaction.

Bolster your self-confidence by constantly saying to yourself, "I want to sell my house, I will sell my house, and I will make money from selling my house". This mantra will guide you and make you

stronger as you go through the motions of the
eventual sale.

Tip 36: Even well-meaning friends can derail
you!

Stay focused. Don't surround yourself with friends
who like to foretell gloom and doom. "You might
regret it," or "There's just too much stress handling
the sale yourself, let the experts do what they're best
at".

These pieces of advice, no matter how well-
intentioned, have no place in your goals. Don't be
easily swayed by what your friends or colleagues tell
you. Refuse to listen to horror stories about meeting
the strangest of strangers.

Chapter 14 Category 5: Getting Serious and Getting Ready

Tip 37: Time to go "pro"

Earlier I provided tips on getting to know your house and going around inside and outside to see what needs to be improved.

Now it's time to closely inspect your home for hidden defects. It's time for a professional inspector. Get him to examine those details that can make or break a deal.

One is the electrical wiring. A fire caused by faulty wiring is serious business. Instead of enjoying the cash from the sale of your house, your hard-earned equity is going towards paying damages and lawyers' fees.

Tip 38: The radon test?

Experts love to mention the radon test. If you run a radon test in your house, this is a huge plus in the eyes of buyers.

The longer the radon tests, the more accurate are its results. High radon levels can be fixed. Always do retests, and provide results to your buyers.

Tip 39: This isn't a multiple choice test.

See to it that the professional inspector or home inspection company you hired provides you with a well written report.

The fill-in-the-blank forms and check boxes type of report may be accurate, but a written, detailed analysis looks better to buyers. It demonstrates to them that you've done your sacred duty as seller.

Tip 40: The well's run dry.

Don't overlook details that can jeopardize the sale or put you in an awkward position later.

If you have a well (most homes out in the far country still have wells!), have this inspected. If you have a written report, show this as well to the buyers.

Tip 41: What's that smell?

If you have a septic system, have a percolation test performed. If repairs are necessary, you either repair them before you sell, or disclose them to the buyers. Don't kill your chances of selling your house because of this detail.

Tip 42: Actually, now that you ask…

Show all repairs in a written report to all prospective buyers. This will eliminate unpleasant surprises later that might delay the sale. Disclosing all house defects and problems will help reduce the time or process leading to the final sale.

Non-disclosure can even cause a re-negotiation of the sale price if the buyers discover the defects themselves. If there is anything you don't want, it's being forced to re-negotiate the price down because of non-disclosure of a fact that you were legally required to disclose.

Tip 43: Show that you mean business!

When the professionals have done their inspections and all reports are in your possession, make copies. You'll want to have as many copies of each report at arm's length, so you're not scampering around for them at the last minute.

Show buyers that you're acting conscientiously and being considerate of their concerns. This will indicate clearly that you're a serious seller and a professional one. Make sure the dates are clearly visible on each and every report.

Tip 44: If I were buying this house…

After you're satisfied that the professional inspectors did their job correctly, act like one. Take one, long last look.

Put on your eagle eyes, and ask yourself; if I were buying this house, what would I want done or repaired?

Tip 45: Is there an expert around?

In terms of repairs and fixes, follow the advice of Bill Effros: there are three categories of things you should fix:

Legally required repairs;
Little things that make a BIG difference;
Big things that make a HUGE difference.

Tip 46: It's the law, sir.

Fix house problems because the law requires you to. These are usually environmental in nature or hidden hazards that can cause health problems for the buyers and their children.

Examples are lead paint and asbestos removal, and harmful insulation material.

Tip 47: You and I are different.

Little things that make a difference are those tasks or jobs that you've somehow delayed or never got around to doing.

Remember that what may be petty to you may not be petty at all to your prospective buyer. No two people think the same way. Selling and buying a house are two different perspectives, two different people, and two different mindsets.

Tip 48: Did you inherit these doorknobs from your grandmother?

Try not to overlook old doorknobs and plates on light switches. If they look lifeless and worn, replace them to liven up the living areas. Try to go for neutral designs.

If your buyers are young, upward mobile professionals, you could go for bolder designs. Make sure that whatever you put on, the buyers can take them off easily should they decide to do so.

Tip 49: That noise is driving me nuts!

Has that leaking faucet been bothering you lately? You can be sure that minor things like leaking faucets can make buyers hesitate.

Faucets that have been leaking for some time demonstrate a homeowner's negligence regarding basic maintenance.

Tip 50: Is this door going to fall on me?

Does your house have doors that sag, don't close properly, squeak or have a knob missing?

There are beautiful ready-made and custom-made doors in your local home centre, so why don't you pay them a visit; get an idea of what kind of doors would breathe life into your house?

Tip 51: So, how many insects do you have here?

What about broken screens that have ugly-looking holes gaping at you and your visitors? A simple thing such as broken screens can be a huge turn off so show consideration for your buyers by taking care of these minor fix-its.

Tip 52: For you or the buyer?

Some experts say that little repairs that can potentially annoy you or your buyers must get fixed.

Getting small, minor jobs done will help increase your chances of selling your house. But getting big things fixed, they say, will only mean profits for the contractor and buyer, not you. This is a matter of personal opinion.

If you take integrity and professionalism to heart, you can proceed with the big repairs and cough up the expense.

Tip 53: Hold your horses!

Here's what some experts are also saying about undertaking major repairs. If it's going to cost you an arm and a leg and substantially reduce the sale price of your home, think twice.

For example, your house costs $200.000.00 in the market. You're thinking of selling it for $250,000.00 to make a neat little profit of $50,000. Repairs will cost you $30,000.00 that reduces your profit to

$20,000. Are the major repairs worth that measly profit?

Crunch some figures before you undertake those major renovations.

Tip 54: I wish you hadn't done that…

Undertaking major renovations may come out of the goodness of your heart, but have you ever thought of looking at the other side of the coin?

What if the potential buyers don't particularly like the renovations you've done, and would have preferred to renovate the house themselves?

When an individual goes out looking to buy a house, that individual is not just buying a physical piece of property but is also thinking of making his future house an extension of his personality and his lifestyle.

So if you're thinking of renovating your house before selling to make it look more presentable, those good intentions may backfire. That's why it's always good to gauge a buyer's plans about your house when he/she first makes contact.

Tip 55: Bring in a contractor.

Some people actually think it's a good idea to bring in a contractor to have a look at their homes after the professional inspection.

Because they know their business inside out, some contractors specialize in preparing homes for sale, and can tell you what should be fixed and what should be left alone.

They can help you save precious dollars. Show them all of the inspection reports. With the contractor's opinion and the home inspection reports in your possession, you should be able to decide what to fix and what not to fix.

Chapter 15: Category 6: Letting the Word Out: "I'm Selling My House!"

Tip 56: Get the word out!

Okay, you've had your house inspected and you've done your own inspection. It's time to let the word out.

You can announce the sale of your house through word of mouth or putting an ad on your paper.

Do an experiment: tell your colleagues at work that you're selling your house. Make a note of the questions they ask. Their questions can serve as an accurate indication of what prospective buyers are also likely to be asking you.

Tip 57: Reach out far and wide!

Your announcement can be published in the national and local community paper. The more people you reach, the more prospects you have. You may also announce in trade papers that are published by real estate associations or the housing authority.

Use as many resources as you can. You have no idea how much more successful you will be in selling when there is a larger audience involved.

You may be slightly inconvenienced by the number of inquiries you'll get, but if you want to sell that house in a hurry, it's a question of statistical proportions.

The more you spread the word around in the media, the more people you reach.

Tip 58: Word of mouth is just as powerful as advertising

Ask your office colleagues to tell their families and friends about your house sale. They may know of people who are moving into the area and looking for homes.

The more colleagues you tell, the more you increase your chances of reaching people you don't even know. After you've told them, follow up after a week and ask if they had any questions about your house that you'd be pleased to clarify. Make it known to them that you're serious about selling, that way they take you seriously and some of them will even want to help you.

Tip 59: Can the company help me?

After you tell your colleagues, speak to the human resources manager of your organization and tell her that if there are executives relocating to your area, you have a house to sell.

You'll never know what the human resources individual can come up with.

Someone may actually be moving to the area to take up a position in your organization; or your human resources manager may have been approached by other human resources professionals from other companies who are desperately looking for houses for their expatriates or returning executives.

Tip 60: Ah, the old reliable…the bulletin board!

Go one step further: use the public bulletin board to post your house sale. Don't forget to leave tabs with your telephone number that can be torn out of the main sheet so that people can call you or pass them on to their friends.

Post a clear picture in color with your ad on the bulletin board. You know how the saying goes; a picture is worth a thousand words.

Tip 61: Am I missing the sugar?

Before you even sit down to word that ad for the papers, think about the ingredients of the recipe for successfully selling of your house.

There are five ingredients you need to have, according to Barb Schwarz, a successful realtor.

Let's take the first ingredient: location. You can't physically uproot your house to take it to a better location. Note that the price of your house must realistically reflect its location.

Tip 62: Have you been negligent?

Second ingredient for a successful sale: Condition. Remember that this is where a professional inspector and a thorough personal inspection by you can make a lot of sense. Schwarz said that the upkeep of the property is a crucial factor in obtaining the highest possible price for a home. Price, like location, must reflect a house's condition.

Tip 63: How much do I want?

Third ingredient: Price. This is the number 1 deciding factor in the sale or no sale of a house. There's a belief among real estate circles that a house is really only worth what a buyer is willing to pay a seller to gain ownership of that house.

Price must have a direct correlation to all the other ingredients for a successful sale. Never mind what the listings or other people say. If your house is overpriced, you won't have any offers, or else it may take a long time to receive offers.

Tip 64: Will the buyer ask for flexibility?

Fourth ingredient: Terms. The more terms you have on the property, the more potential purchasers you reach. Again, the price of your house must reflect the kinds of terms available to purchase it.

Tip 65: Is this a good time to sell?

Fifth ingredient: Market. Market conditions are influenced by key factors such as interest rates, supply and demand of houses in your area, competition and the general state of the economy.

Real estate is a cyclical phenomenon. The beginning of 2000 witnessed a surge in home building. All of a sudden homes were being sold faster than contractors could build them. When there's a real estate boom, this is an excellent opportunity to make a killing!

Tip 66: The truth will come out…

So keep those five ingredients uppermost in your mind at all times. Now you're ready to word that ad.

Be honest. Don't say you have a house in excellent condition when your inspection report has a long list of deficiencies and repairs your house will require.

Don't say you have 3 full bathrooms when you really have only two bathrooms and one powder room. A powder room, as we all know, does not qualify as a full bathroom.

Also, don't say that you live in a quiet neighborhood when in fact your house is located near a university campus where you hear students partying all night. If you mention that your house has an alarm system, it better work.

Tip 67: Umm, how will I word this ad?

If you aren't good with words, that is, it's taking you painstakingly long to draft an ad, go with ads placed in the local and regional papers that you FEEL works for you.

This means putting yourself in the buyer's shoes: you read the ad, it makes you curious, and you take down the number. If an ad pleases you or strikes you as effective and persuasive, copy the style and content of the ad.

Another alternative would be to refer back to some of the books you read on successful real estate sales and mull over the model ads.

Tip 68: Can you just state the bottom line please?

When you're ready to write out an ad, clarity and brevity must be your parameters. If your price is reasonable and realistic and you put the ad in the right strategic places, you'll get at least 20 calls.

Tip 69: Do your thinking before picking up that phone

Don't do what many people do. They call the classified ads department of their local and regional papers and craft the ad with the person in the other line.

Don't waste time by providing information only while you're on the phone. Instead, figure everything out in advance.

And when we say everything, we mean that by the time you call the classified ads person, you know ahead of time what your ad will look like, what it will say, where to put it, what abbreviations to use and whether or not it should have a border (experts say you don't need a fancy border for your ad to catch the readers' attention).

Bill Effros who sold his house in five days said that you don't need a double column or a fancy border for your ad.

Tip 70: Wait and see.

Be careful about how long you want your ad to run. An ad that's been around too long will give readers the impression that your house is not selling because of major problems. It will also tell them that maybe buyers are coming to see the house only to walk away disappointed.

Some experts say a five-day ad is sufficient. If you don't get a sufficient number of serious callers, pull out the ad, wait a few weeks, and start all over again. Review the ad's wording. Perhaps there's something in the ad that doesn't sound right that you didn't notice the first time.

Tip 71: Where should I publish?

Put it in two sure places where it will get read. Again, pretend you're the buyer looking for a house. Where would you most likely look? That's the section where you should place your ad.

Your local paper with a small circulation and your regional paper with a much larger circulation should be your target destinations for your ad.

Tip 72: One is enough.

Buyers often don't really want to buy 4-5 newspapers to look for houses for sale. They'd much rather concentrate on one paper and encircle the ads that could lead to potential visits. They usually go for the paper which is the most popular with the highest number of readers. That's the paper where your ad must also go.

Tip 73: Cyberspace? Do I really want Martians buying my house?

What about placing my ad on the Internet, you ask? If our guess of the human tendency is right, people may look at the Internet for houses for sale, but may not necessarily be serious buyers.

So the Internet for now would be an alternative to traditional newspaper advertising. Just watch people in cafes who are reading the classified ads. They usually mark the paper, circling those ads that they're interested in.

On the Internet, the buyer would either copy contact details by hand or print the ad; this can be cumbersome. At least with the newspaper at hand, people can just toss it in the seat of their cars as they drive off to visit the property, and can look at the ad again, if needed.

Tip 74: Do you want to write a house story? Try the home section, not the classified ads

Think twice, even three times before you get that pencil or word processor moving. Avoid flowery words. Avoid expressions like "it will capture your heart", or "a house of your dreams", or "here's a house where you can have many memorable days".

People are not really looking for something to captivate their hearts or memories. They're looking for a real house to live in, for a roof over their heads. The dreams and memories can come later, but at this point, buyers are only interested in a physical structure that they claim ownership of.

Tip 75: What should I say?

Word your ad so that it answers the questions that buyers would want to know: location, the fact that you're selling it yourself (no brokers or agents please), brief description of house, a starting reasonable price. Mention that you'll take the best reasonable offer, and put your area code and telephone number. These are the only points that buyers are initially interested in. Other details like amenities and extras and true value can be discussed face to face or during a follow-up telephone call.

Tip 76: This is EXACTLY how I want it

Bill Effros recommends that your ad should be positioned as follows: location, upper top left and "BY OWNER" right hand side top.

Type of house (condo, duplex, cottage, etc) on the next line. Brief description of major feature on the following line.

Then your starting price, e.g. "$150,000 or best reasonable offer" on the next line, to be followed by inspection times (e.g. Sat-Sun 10-5).

Last line on low bottom left, the words: HIGHEST BIDDER", and your telephone number beside it.

Note: your ad is meant to give you as many callers as possible. Details about the property can be provided to them on the phone if they request them. And to play safe, email or fax the copy of the ad exactly as you want it to appear in the paper. You could be dealing with an ad taker who is taking ads for the first time and may not understand what "flush left" or "flush left" mean.

Tip 77: Screen calls.

If you're a busy person with a full time job, you may want to filter your calls. Before you call the paper to have your ad put, make sure you set yourself up with an answering machine or an answering service.

You don't want to be called in the middle of the night or at meal times to answer questions about your house and be forced to make a visit appointment. With an answering machine, you decide who you want to call back.

You will also be able to tell who the serious buyers are versus the frivolous ones. People who leave their names and numbers and are brief in their message make a good impression.

You want to avoid receiving callers who talk incessantly or ask questions the answers of which are already in the ad.

Be wary of people who also try to negotiate the price down over the phone without even asking to see the property.

This should raise your antennas to the fact that one, they probably can't afford the price to begin with, or second, they can't get their bank to finance that amount.

Tip 78: Add "Or best reasonable offer"

A famous real estate writer says that it's not so much the description of the property that will get you a sufficient number of callers; it is the stated price on your ad.

If it is within their price range, they will call. If not, they'll go on to the next ad. So make sure you don't omit this detail but add, "or best reasonable offer."

Tip 79: It's my favorite day of the week!

Only you will pick the days you want your ad to appear. The approach is to reach as many readers as possible. In the United States, Sundays are when the ads run in the hundreds, and in Canada, Saturday has the highest number of readers. Wednesday is also ad day in Canada but to a lesser extent than Saturday. Don't let the ad taker convince you to put your ad on certain days of the week. Go with what you know and what common practice is.

Bear in mind that unless people are really looking for something particular in the paper, they don't look at the paper during the week.

They are more relaxed during weekends and are likely to pick up the paper from the kitchen table. For anxious buyers however, they deliberately read the papers every morning with the hope that they find the "house of their dreams".

Tip 80: Would you repeat that please?

Once your ad is published, buy the paper and read your ad a few times, ensuring that all details are correctly listed.

Look at your phone number and make sure it was listed correctly. Do not forget to list your area code.

The same city may have two different area codes; one for the east end district and another for the west end side of town. You could lose hundreds of potential buyers with this omission.

Tip 81: How do I sound?

So the ad has been placed. Brace yourself for calls! They will increase in number as people read your ad and then pass it off to friends and family.

Rehearse your lines. You'll want to give the impression that you're a serious seller, so you expect the same from them as buyers.

Don't panic if you're getting too many calls or none at all on the first day. Take a deep breath and get ready for the avalanche. While having an answering machine is a good idea for the sake of filtering serious callers from the frivolous, it's perfectly alright for you to take the call yourself if you feel like it.

Tip 82: Take it down

Have pen and paper ready. Take down each caller's name and number. Jot down their questions. This will give you an idea of future questions, and you'll know how to answer them properly the next time.

Tip 83: Are you a (phone) grouch?

When you answer calls, come across as friendly. The impression you DON'T want to give is that of a tired, harassed seller who's sick and tired of answering questions on the phone.

Practice basic courtesy. Be professional. And sound like one!

Tip 84: Let's get serious here.

Here's an important tip: if you get 25 calls by the third day, your ad worked. Getting 25 calls means that 25 people read your ad and dialed your number.

Don't expect 25 buyers though. Callers and buyers are two separate people.

Chapter 16: Category 7: Showing Your Home

Tip 85: It bothers me...

When buyers come to visit, make sure there is nothing about your house that will distract them. Make sure the entrance door is clean, and if it's winter time, make sure the snow has been cleared.

Ensure that the entranceway is well lit and doesn't look in disarray. Remove coats and other clothing from their field of vision, no skis by the doorway, no ball or other play objects that may obstruct the path or cause them to trip over. A buyer who trips in your house is a terrible way to start.

Tip 86: Dust collectors.

Buyers must feel that the seller has taste and class. Get rid of clutter before their visit. Dust collecting trophies and souvenir items bought during trips can make an ugly sight especially if they're too close to one another without any order and are thick with dust!

Tip 87: Surround yourself with beauty.

Of course be old-fashioned: good lights and flowers would be nice (not too much though – your buyer could be allergic to flower scents).

Tip 88: I knew you'd ask that!

Putting up signs to answer frequent questions can save you time. It's also an efficient way to let you give the tour without being interrupted too many times.

Signs can include things like: condo fees are $150.00 per month, appliances, fixtures and draperies are included with the sale, garage and garden equipment are included, china not included, there are 8 phone jacks on the first floor and 3 on the second floor, there is a wireless connection, shelves are included, etc.

Tip 89: Children OK, animals NO!

Get your pets out of the way. You won't know in advance who is allergic to dogs and cats. Plus the barking of dogs and the meowing of cats can be very distracting, and an annoyance for non-pet lovers.

Tip 90: Who's that standing by the door?

Before buyers come, it's good to have a closer. The closer should be clearly visible to buyers, and should be near the door so he/she can keep track of buyers who arrive and leave the property.

The closer can usually tell by your instincts who are the interested buyers. When the closer asks if they want to know how the bidding process works, those who are not interested will simply say no and leave.

Chapter 17: Category 8: Negotiations, Settlement and Contract

Tip 91: Can we talk about your price?

You can be 99% sure that buyers will negotiate to bring the price down; this is why houses are sold and bought as a result of negotiations, which could take days, if you're lucky, or longer, if you meet buyers who really want your house but don't want to pay the price you're asking for.

It's curious what kind of arguments buyers will come up with to convince you to lower your price. "But your backyard needs a lot of tending"; "The kitchen tiles are not in good shape and we'd have to replace them ourselves"; or "But your house is near a cemetery (or a prison or a quarry), who'd want to buy your house?"

Don't let buyers run you and your house down. If you want to unburden yourself quickly of your property because you've got an important trip scheduled or you need to make a counteroffer on another property, then by all means lower your price.

However, if you're convinced that your property is worth more (based on the offers you've received so far), then be firm with your price.

Buyers will always take advantage of those situations where you show a little hesitation about the price. Tell them your price is final and that you're not prepared to negotiate.

Tip 92: It doesn't hurt to be honest.

When negotiations begin, remember that honesty is still the best policy. There is this great temptation to get greedy and you bid against your buyers. Don't. You may end up still owning your house months later because the bidders couldn't keep up with the price.

The more important consideration for you is not how much extra thousands of dollars you can get above your original price, but if you're a decent person, your number one concern should be who, among these buyers, will pay me for what I asked for and take good care of my house the way I did?

Tip 93: My home is your home now

Once you've found a buyer for your home and all the terms have been negotiated to both parties' satisfaction, the next step is to transfer ownership of the house. Since you're on your own, you'll need to initiate the paper work yourself.

This is where the government can help you. The US Department of Housing and Urban Development has published a book entitled "Settlement Costs". It is free and contains valuable guidelines on settlement matters (the booklet title may have changed, check with your city government).

From this publication, you'll be able to decide who to consult with in terms of the different steps of the closing process. You will need a lawyer (or notary), or an escrow company or your bank. Settlement procedures vary from state to state and from country to country.

Tip 94: How quickly will he settle this matter for me?

After you have chosen your settlement agent, get the name of the settlement agent of your buyer and provide this to your own agent.

The way it works is the two agents will then work together to contact the banks, arrange for title searches and title insurance, draw up the sale contract and calculate any other fees that have to be paid.

Settlement agents don't work with the same speed as other agents. If you feel that the process has stalled and it's not your agent's fault, then your buyer's agent may be causing the delays. If delays become major concerns, you may want to seriously consider the next buyer on your list, but inform the first buyer that you can't afford to wait any longer.

Tip 95: This covers just about everything

When settlement details are finalized, a contract is drawn up. The contract must include the following details:
   a. Amount/location of property
   b. Timing of the sale

c. Transfer of funds
d. Items included in, and excluded from, the sale
e. Conveyance of title
f. Apportionment of fees to be paid
g. Insurance matters

And other such things that are typically part of a sale contract for private property. If there are any clauses that you don't understand, have your lawyer explain them to you. Ask questions until you're satisfied that everything is crystal clear.

Tip 96: Can we change this a little bit?

Be prepared for requests from the buyer to modify parts of the contract. Don't verbally agree to anything until your lawyer confirms that the requested changes are in order.

This part of the exercise may take longer than you expected. Lawyers are shrewd creatures and will make every attempt to get the most for their clients. They're only doing their job, and they're doing what they're best at; arguing and haggling.

It is up to your lawyer to defend your interests so hopefully, the lawyer you hired is as sharp and shrewd as your buyer's lawyer.

When contract discussions are going on, ask your lawyer's opinion as to the advantages and disadvantages of agreeing or disagreeing with a particular clause. Discuss potential consequences and how changing a clause could jeopardize your rights as a seller.

And if you do agree to change a clause, ensure that all changes are put in writing either within the body of the contract or as an addendum.

Tip 97: About that money…

Ask your lawyer about asking for a down payment from the buyer. Some contracts require it to protect the seller: This down payment will usually make the buyer live up to his commitment to buy the property within a reasonable amount of time.

This down payment is called "earnest money" by some people. It morally obliges the buyer to finalize a mortgage with his bank, to have the property inspected within a reasonable period and to be prepared to settle by a certain date.

This down payment is not refunded back to the buyer should the sale not take place. Down payments may range from $1,000 to as much as 10% of the purchase price and is kept in escrow by your settlement agent.

Tip 98: Crossing the t's and dotting the i's…

As soon as all paperwork is final and parties are ready to sign the contract, the settlement (also called closing in some parts of Canada) takes place in either of the following places: the settlement agent's office, bank, insurance office, or anywhere where you and the buyer and your respective agents agree to meet and sign papers.

This is the day you will probably get the biggest cash windfall in your life, and when someone else takes ownership of your house.

You can start breathing normally again when that check lands on your hands, and you and your personal effects are physically out of your house!

Tip 99: What, you've changed your mind?

Expect last minute surprises. A deal can be called off because:

The buyer could not get financing and has no money of his own. Something went wrong with the title search or an insurance detail was not dealt with. Someone suddenly is afraid and wants to back out, or some personal emergencies like a sudden death in the family or terminal illness; are forcing the parties not to go through with the deal.

Whatever happens, just make sure you're not walking up the path towards financial ruin.

Tip 100: You're willing to pay more for my house?

When you put an ad for your house, and the price looks reasonable to the pool of buyers that are out there, you'll get end buyers.

End buyers are buyers who are looking to buy a house to live in.

You'll also get professional buyers; they include real estate brokers looking for homes to buy, builders specializing in remodeling and reselling homes or developers who want to buy the property because of the land.

Don't be afraid of the professional buyers, because they know the true value of your house. They'll push the bidding price higher because they know what they're doing, and by pushing up the price, they weed off the end buyers who eventually drop out because the price is beyond their budget.

If a professional buyer offers you a price for your house that will make you happy, then by all means, go with the professional buyer.

Tip 101: Weeding out the curious.

If after you place your ad, you get 100 calls, don't let that make you comfortable thinking that your house is going to be sold immediately.

The truth is, of those 100 calls, less than half are serious buyers. Or half of them want your home but don't have the means to buy it.

Of that bunch, there is only one truly qualified buyer, and that qualified buyer is the one who can deliver the cash when it's time to deliver it. The other 99 are just "probably" buyers.

Chapter 18: Conclusion

These tips have served as your starter kit. You'll now need to make a decision about whether you still want to go solo. Many have done so; and after they've sold their first house, they wouldn't hesitate to do it again!

Knowledge is power, that's how the classic adage goes. And it's more meaningful when you're selling your house. Soldiers don't go to combat without orders, plans, maps and guns.

Entrepreneurs don't create businesses that will one day flourish without prior knowledge of the product or service they want to peddle.

Surgeons don't go into the operating room without knowledge of their patient; his disease and the drugs he's taking.

As a first time seller, these 101 tips are your ammunition, your basic knowledge. And it's up to you to use them to your advantage. You want this experience to be a win-win situation.

After all, part of your worth as a human being is tied to your house. Your property is a reflection of the long years of hard work and savings you've put into it.

If you're about to sell your house and the market is still hot you'll have that cash windfall you've always dreamed of. Your house will make you rich. So I hope you've taken good care of it.

When you sign those settlement papers, it's your house's turn to take care of you.

Good Luck!

www.ingramcontent.com/pod-product-compliance
Lightning Source LLC
Chambersburg PA
CBHW051720170526
45167CB00002B/742